In Their Nightgowns, Dancing

A Play

by Michael Armstrong

In Their Nightgowns, Dancing

A Play

by Michael Armstrong

UNBC Press
Prince George, BC
2005

Canadian Cataloguing in Publication Data

Armstrong, Michael, 1955-

In their nightgowns, dancing / Michael Armstrong.

A play.

ISBN 1-896315-16-X

I. Title.

PS8551.R76386I5 2005 C812'.54 C2005-904260-5

Design: Kyle Thompson, Rob Budde, Lynda Williams

Editor: Rob Budde

Cover Photos: Ken White

UNBC Press

3333 University Way

Prince George BC Canada

V2N 4Z9

For Rumiana

"Siehe, wir lieben nicht, wie die Blumen, aus einem einzigen Jahr..."

Die Dritte Elegie, RANIER MARIA RILKE

Introduction

This play has been six years in the making. An early draft of In Their Nightgowns, Dancing, directed by the playwright, was performed in Prince George and Toronto in the summer and fall of 1999. Under the dramaturgy and direction of Peg Christoperson, it was remounted in Vancouver in the summer of 2000 at the UBC Summer Theatre Festival. Both of these versions were two-handers with Michael Armstrong and Rumiana Cormack playing Aslan and Irena. In September 2001, the play was workshopped at the Banff playRites Colony.

In the fall of 2003, the play was rewritten in a form very close to its present one; and in the spring of 2004, Roughhouse Theatre Project of Prince George mounted a production for Theatre BC's Central Interior Zone Festival with the following cast and production team. It went on to win a number of awards at Theatre BC's Mainstage Festival and represented BC at the Canada West Play Festival in Prince Albert, Saskatchewan, in October of that year.

Michael Armstrong Aslan
Rumiana Cormack Irena

Chorus

Katherine Trepanier

Chorus, Katja, Exile, Mariena, Anya, Stalin Aide, Postal Worker, Russian Woman, Citizen, Russian Soldier, Tourist, Rude Girl, Inge, Stroller

David Quast

Chorus, Red Army, Child, Mr. Hrusinsky, Rudy, Kolya, Stalin Aide, Lover, Russian Occupier, Official, Lenin, Citizen, Jozef, Russian Guard, Yevgeny, Consular, Dock Worker, Husband

Wayne Empey

Chorus, Exile, Child, Mr. Chocena, Aslan's Father, Stalin, Krushchev, Soup Man, Irena's Father, Lindegard, Stroller, Political Officer, Citizen, Soldier, Border German, Doctor, Dock Worker, Vaclav Havel

Andrea Mallett

Chorus, Aslan's Mother, Child, Mrs. Caslavska, Babka, Anya's Mother, Minister in Charge, Russian Woman, Citizen, Irena's Mother, Tourist, Border Crosser, Rude Girl

Directed by Allison Haley
Set Design by Phil Morrison
Costumes by Pat Jorgensen
Lights by Ken White
Stage Manager Dominic Maguire
An original score was composed and performed live on cello by Jordan Dyck.

I would like to acknowledge several invaluable sources, which led to the creation of this work. I am grateful for the beautiful translations of Rainer Maria Rilke's poems by Stephen Mitchell, which are available in several editions from Random House and Shambhala. I would also like to thank Viktor Suvorov for his book, The Liberators: My Life in the Soviet Army (W.W. Norton and Co, 1981.)

In the fall of 1998, I met a man at a poetry reading in a Calgary book store. He was from a southern Russian republic, spoke five languages and had served in the army that had invaded Czechoslovakia. He inspired the character of Aslan. He also bought me a glass of wine. I didn't catch his name. Thank you.

Many people offered support and suggestions in the early stages of this script. I would like to thank, particularly, Robin Mossley, Kevin Kerr, and Peg Christopherson. I would like to thank Theatre BC for their support and encouragement and for the many opportunities they provide for community theatre in this province.

I would like to acknowledge the assistance of the 2001 Banff playRites Colony - a partnership between the Canada Council for the Arts, The Banff Centre for the Arts, and Alberta Theatre Projects.

A special thank you to my dramaturge and mentor in Banff, John Murrell.

Most importantly, however, I am deeply indebted to Josef and Irina Vitko for their willingness to share their story and their permission to me to reshape it. And of course, I can not begin to express my gratitude to their daughter, Rumiana. Ja ťa lubím. Her story is Irena's story.

Much of what you will read is true.

Characters

Irena

Irena is a dark haired woman in her mid-forties. Perhaps she has an accent, perhaps not; it is hard to tell. She has been in this country for a long time and has worked hard to blend in. She has been an English teacher for many years. She has had a place in the world but has recently been shaken from it. She is in mid-leap. She is speaking to her daughter who is perhaps 17 or 18 years old.

Aslan

Aslan is a man in his late-fifties with dark brown or black hair, streaked with gray. He tries to look neat but is always a little unkempt, as though a certain wildness resides in him and bleeds through all his attempts at formal disguise. He speaks many languages well and has a slight, indefinable, Eastern European accent. Words lay restless on his tongue. He enjoys the discoveries of speaking. He has an ironic, sometimes bitter, sense of humour. He is speaking to his son who is in his early 30's.

They are Canadians. They are immigrants. They are our neighbours. We do not know them as well as we should.

Chorus

The chorus that appears at the beginning and ending of this story also play all of the small roles that appear throughout the body of the play. I suggest a chorus of four, two men and two women, of differing ages; actors capable of playing a diverse range of roles.

The Setting

The stories unfold in a city on the Canadian prairie. The characters are neither in the same place nor the same time; though, in both cases, it is very close to the present.

Irena is in her home, packing.

Aslan is on a path beside the river that flows through the city.

A Note on Format

In form, the play moves back and forth from the colloquial to the poetic. The structure of the text often reflects this. The punctuation and line lengths are reflective of rhythm and breath and can be used as a guide to the actors and director. Both characters have a tendency to move toward the poetic in times of passion or deep memory. There is a certain commonality to the deeper voice from which these passages arise. This is a play about memory and discovery. How intimately they are linked.

ACT ONE

Part One: Openings

As the lights fade up on the stage, we hear a children's chorus singing in Slovak. As they sing, Irena enters with an arm full of clothing and papers and packs a suitcase that is sitting open on the stage. She is left holding a photograph.

Šípky naše sledujem
K dveram neznamym
S mojim klučom magickym
Otvoriť sa ich odvažim.

Irena
continuing and finishing the song alone
Šípky Šípky
Who are we?
(Then she speaks.) Now you have to tell us who we are so we can play our game.

Chorus
She knows this song.

Irena
Oh, you scared me. I had no idea you were there.

Chorus
What does it mean?

Irena

The song?
We will follow our arrow
to a mysterious door.
With our magical key
we will try to open it.
It's just a children's song from Czechoslovakia.

Chorus

Why are you packing?

Irena

I'm leaving.

Chorus

Leaving?

Irena

I'm going to my brother's for a while. Till I get my own place.

Chorus

No.

Irena

You can stay here with your father if you'd like, or you can come with me. Whatever you'd like.

Chorus

Shh. Shh. Shh. *(These sounds are imperative, blocking out. Irena has to speak her next line over them.)*

Irena

You weren't home. I was going to talk to you when you got home. You haven't been home much.

Chorus

She is angry. It's been easier to be out.

Irena

I know. It's been pretty ugly around here these past few weeks. I'm sorry.

Chorus

(A collective sigh. A collapse.) She is lost. Lost.

Irena

Oh, my girl. This is not about you. I'm not leaving you.

Chorus

The room swirls around her.

Irena

Come in. Sit down. *(She removes the suitcase from the chair and turns it to face the audience.)* Please.

Lights shift to Aslan.

Chorus

Aslan.

Aslan

Yes.

Chorus

Illya.

Aslan

Illya?

Chorus

Your son.

Aslan

My son. *(He is stunned.)*
My son.
(He almost whispers.) Tote kinder wollten zu dir.

Chorus

What is that?

Aslan

I'm sorry. It's just a line from one of Rilke's poems.
You have taken me by surprise. I don't know what to say.

Chorus

He is nervous too.

Aslan

How did you find me?

Chorus

They told him at the university that you walked here often. By the river.

Aslan

I mean...how did you know I lived here? In this city. This country.
How did you even know I was still alive?
I had no idea you would come after me. When I left you, you were an infant in your mother's arms. Staring after me as I climbed the gangplank. And now...psht...you are a man.

Chorus

It has been a long journey. You were not easy to find.

Aslan

No. It has been many years and the trail is long and

restless. My life has not been linear or logical like the world Plato desired. Free of the madness of poets.

Chorus

He has not read Plato.

Aslan

I am sorry. I have moved often from place to place. From language to language. Capriciously almost. My life is a little like this river at our feet. Always moving forward.

Chorus

Why have you moved so often?

Aslan

I have been looking for something. The right words I think. The right story.

Chorus

What do you mean?

Aslan

Every language describes the world in a different way. It grows up seeking to explain itself. Its place in the world. Listen to the river.

Chorus

(Whispering as the river, as Aslan speaks.) Shh. Shh. Shh.

Aslan

It whispers its own name. Intimate whispers. Of the river bank and the sky. The shining fish slipping through it. In winter it murmurs in dreams beneath the ice. Prays for rebirth. The sudden penetration of spring light. A fresh wind like fingers. A belly of warm mud.

(The whispering ends.)
With every language I have learned, I have hoped to find the words to explain who I am. Where I belong.

Chorus
Did you not belong with him? With his mother.

Aslan
I thought so for a time. But we all of us speak a different language. If we do not listen carefully, we will misunderstand. Your mother and I could not grasp the basic metaphors that defined one another.

Chorus
That is confusing.

Aslan
You're right. That is confusing. How can I explain better? Every word is a story. A metaphor. It roots us to the earth, to the real, through a series of ideas. The word 'decant' for instance comes from the Greek kanthos, meaning corner of the eye. It is how a poet saw the wine pouring from the jug like tears from the corners of his eye.
Our languages, our selves, are built from a thousand such stories. But the stories are different and sometimes they do not translate. What if there was no wine where you came from? You might not understand.
I could not explain myself to your mother. I was young. I had no idea who I was. I did not yet have the words.
I have been looking for them.

Chorus
Do you have them now?

Aslan
Perhaps. That is why you are here, isn't it? It is a story you

are missing too. You want to know who I am. Where you come from.

Chorus
Yes.

Aslan
I have not spoken of these things for a long time. I have spent so much more energy moving away than looking back.

Chorus
Look back for him now. He is close. You can see the hunger in his eyes

Aslan
I don't know.

Chorus
Look back for him.
Aslan is frightened by the idea. The light shifts back to Irena and the chorus follows.

Chorus
Shh.

Irena
Your father's a good man. Sometimes I think I'm an idiot.

Chorus
Your fingers in her hair.

Irena
He was in my first year English class. He sat in front of me. His blonde hair hung over his shirt collar in little curls. I wanted to twirl his hair in my fingers.

When he first asked me out, he was very formal. He said,

Chorus

I would be pleased if you would join me for a drink.

Irena

He said, I would be pleased.
I don't think I'd ever heard anyone speak like that before.
I'd be honoured, I said.
And I was.

Chorus

She's confused. Why are you leaving?

Irena

I'm not sure I can explain that to you.
I feel like I've spent the last thirty years trying to be someone else.
I tried very hard to make this work. This marriage. This family. It's what I'm supposed to do. Going to university. Meeting your father. Getting married. Teaching year after year. But sometimes, when we live in the world in a logical manner, we become dead to the magic and poetry that swirl around us.

Chorus

She doesn't understand.

Irena

No. No, you don't.
As we grow older we are constantly becoming and becoming. New stories awakening. Old ones lost. Our lost stories sometimes lie in ambush around us and one day, without any real warning, they leap up and force us to fight for our lives.

This photograph. It's the apartment I lived in before we left Czechoslovakia. Mami and Tato took it on their trip back to Europe. The stories in here have wrestled me to the ground.

Chorus

Hush.
Listen.
We are ready.
Tell us your story now.
His story.
Her story.
Our story.
Who are we?

Part Two: Journeys

Mother

They came for us in the middle of the night. *(The Red Army brutally ushers her on to the stage.)* It was November,

Aslan

my mother said,

Mother

winter coming. They woke us up. Herded us onto trains at gunpoint and took us away.
Your brother died on that train. In the boxcar. He was buried beside the track. He was two.

Aslan

His name was also Illya.

Mother

You were born two months later.

Aslan

I think my mother survived because she was pregnant. A woman, pregnant, is about as indestructible as we get. She told me later,

Mother

I wanted to die. *(The Red Army exits.)*

Aslan

She said,

Mother

I didn't die because you wouldn't let me. You insisted on being born. I could hear you cursing in the womb. This was a good sign.

Aslan

1943. Stalin cleared out the Caucasus. *(The Red Army ushers in two other exiles. They join Mother and huddle together.)*

Mother

He deported the Chechens,

Exile One

the Ingush,

The Red Army

the Karachi, *(He stands checking his lists.)*

Exile Two

the Balkars,

Mother

almost two million of us,

Aslan

to Kazakhstan and Kyrgyzia. (*The Red Army pushes Mother toward Aslan. She looks him in the eye as she speaks.)*

Mother

One out of every four of us died on the trains. In the boxcars. *(She retreats upstage.)*

Aslan

Exiles.

There is evil everywhere.
We lived on a shit farm with other exiles. In the winter it was cold as hell. In the summer it was hot and dry and the dust blew over us like a disease. (*Katja is pushed by the Red Army toward Aslan. She looks him in the eye.)* My sister, Katja, and I were not even allowed to go to school.

Katja
We are peasants. *(She retreats upstage.)*

Aslan
In the Soviet Union they had a law against peasants.

A Man
Fucking Pig.

Aslan
The Kazakhs hated us. We came from nowhere. We ate their food. We lived on their land. The glorious Red Army guarded us. *(The man is pushed toward Aslan.)* We must be criminals.

A Man
They treat us like criminals.

The Red Army
Move along. *(He pushes the man upstage and resumes his guard duty. The Exiles dream of revenge.)*

Aslan
Maybe we are criminals. *(There is a glint in his eye.)*
It's more interesting than nobody.
Whole nations of criminals. Dangerous criminals.
Dangerous enough to be murdered, deported, guarded for thirteen years. The Sinister Peoples of the Caucasus.
Always ready to put a knife in Russia's back.

(There is a vicious stabbing. A man, an exile or the son of an exile, puts his knife into the back of the Army. He works it in, holding the soldier upright until he is sure it is done. He lets the soldier fall off the knife which is revealed dripping with blood. He spits on the corpse. The others strip the boots and coat off the corpse.)

I read in the newspapers about Chechnya. The battles with Russia. Holding the entire Russian nation by the throat.
We are still criminals.
Here's to the criminals.

Bury that knife, brothers.
Bury it deep.
(All exit. On his way off, Aslan steps over the body, which remains on the stage.)

Irena

(Children run out onto the stage. The body rises to join them. Irena and Mariena run out together giggling. They are dressed the same.)
When we were little girls in Bratislava, my best friend Mariena and I knew how to be cute. We practiced. We would do our hair the same. We would wear the same clothes. We would stand in front of the mirror.
(Like twins, they smile, clasp their hands in front of themselves and squirm like little girls.)
When you know how to be cute, you can get away with a lot.
There was a game we would play on the streets in front of our apartment. Or inside on rainy days. It was called Šípky.

The Little Children

Šípky!

Irena

That's Slovak for arrows. It was a game of magical destinies.

Mariena

Magic!

The Children

Ohhh.

Irena

We would always start downstairs at the front door of the apartment building. We would throw our arrow up in to the air spinning. When it landed, we would go where it pointed.
Across the lobby. *(The little children run across the stage.)*
Up a stair. *(They run again.)*
Down a hallway. (*And again.*)
A door. (*They stand with Irena, expectant. Someone knocks.*)
When the door opened, we would sing,

Mariena and Irena *(singing)*

Šípky naše sledujem
K dveram neznamym
S mojim klučom magickym
Otvorit˘ sa ich odvažim.

All The Children

Šípky, šípky
We have the key.
Šípky, šípky
Who are we?

Mariena

Now you have to tell us who we are so we can play our game.

Irena

We would be oh sooo cute that they would have to play with us. They would have to make up imaginary characters for us to be. Then they would have to make up an imaginary place for us to play in.

Some people didn't have much imagination. Mr. Chočena, our mailman.

(One by one the children peel off to become the other characters until only Mariena and Irena are left with Mr. Hrusinsky.)

The Children

Mr. Chočena! Mr. Chočena!

Mr. Chočena

I'm busy. I'm busy. *(He relents.)* Ok, ok. I'll look in my bag. *(Mr. Chočena pulls out a letter from his mail bag and consults it.)* You are farmers from Chotebuz. Now go! *(He exits.)*

Children

Farmers?!

Irena

But, in my apartment building, where people knew our game better, there were some who would have fun with us.

Mrs. Caslavska, the old woman on the fourth floor.

Mrs. Caslavska

Deti, deti! You are all wonderful members of the

Czechoslovakian Olympic Team. You have gone to Mexico to win medals for our country. Come in. Come in. I will give you medals. I will give you tea. *(She exits.)*

Irena
Or Mr. Hrusinsky.

Mr. Hrusinsky
We are three sisters, famous actresses on the Moscow stage. The Czar's son has fallen in love with one of us and we must meet with him secretly to find out whom he favours. This note will tell us where the meeting will be. We will wear hats as a disguise. *(He exits with Mariena.)*

Irena
Mrs. Caslavska.
Mr. Hrusinsky.
Somehow, our arrow led us to them over and over again. Many more times then chance should allow. There was a certain magic in it.

Aslan and Irena
As a child

Aslan
I spoke only three languages;

Irena
I took two kinds of journeys;

Aslan
Kazakh

Irena

The secret ones

Aslan

Chechen

Irena

And the family ones.

Aslan

And Russian because my father insisted.

Father

(Crossing the stage.) Stalin will die someday.

Aslan

He was an optimist.

Irena

Both of my parents taught at the university so twice a year we would go on vacation.

Aslan

As I grew up, I made friends with another boy. Rudy. He was a Balkar.

Rudy

(Rudy enters and raises his hand, tentatively, in greeting.) Merhaba! *(Hello.)*

Aslan

He spoke Turkish. So I learned that too.

Voice Off

Rudy!

Rudy

Yarin görüþmek üzere. *(See you tomorrow.)*

(He exits.)

Aslan

Ýnþallah.

If God wills.

My mother started an illegal school for exile children. I translated for him.

We loved school. It was a break from the fields.

Irena

In the winter,

Aslan

In the spring,

Irena

we went skiing.

Aslan

there were birds. Ducks. Flying overhead in formation. Momma said they were flying home. *(She enters and goes to Aslan.)*

Mother

Look, Aslan! Look! See the ducks flying home. Such a long way. Over the plains to the Caspian Sea. Over the sea to home. Watch the birds, Aslan. That is where we will go. One day.

Irena

In the summer, we would always go to Bulgaria. First to Sofia, to visit my grandmother, my Babka. Then on to the Black Sea. Babka never came with us.

I would take her face in my hands.

Come to the beach with me Babka.

Babka

Ne, ne, tova neje za mene vece, Rena. *(It is too late for me, Irena.)* I am too old for the beach. In the hot sun, I would dry up and blow away. But, bring me back a thimbleful of sand to add to my hourglass. *(Irena takes Babka's arm and together they exit.)*

Aslan

One day, Rudy and I we went away. *(Rudy enters with a small rucksack.)* I think we were running away. That's what I told my sister, Katja, the morning we left. Anyway, we were gone overnight. I remember we walked and walked.

We took some food. *(Rudy hands him two potatoes.)* I took two potatoes. Rudy took an onion and some bread. *(Rudy holds them up proudly.)* We ate the bread and half the onion. *(Rudy takes a bite of the onion.)* We threw the potatoes at some cows. *(They throw them.)*

That evening we climbed a big hill covered with grass. We stood on the top and looked into the setting sun and imagined we could see water. Imagined the Caspian Sea. You could see a long way from that hill but you can't see that far. When you are a little boy, though, you can see much farther than a man. We thought we saw the sun glinting off the Caspian Sea just before it set.

As we stood, staring intently into the sunset toward a home neither of us had ever seen, ducks came flying over us. *(The birds appear upstage, flying, and begin to move downstage toward the boys.)* They came from the east and they came in formation and they were calling their harsh duck calls and they swept over us by what seemed like only inches. It was probably more than that but we were so tall that evening, Rudy and I, taller than you can

imagine, and when the ducks came we stood among them as they passed and we spread our wings and flew with them, yelling. *(They fly in unison with the ducks for a while, crying out with a desparate joy, and then the ducks begin to retreat upstage again.)* We flew over the grass, over the hills, over the plains, over the sea to home, over the sea to home. We ran with our arms outstretched, yelling at the top of our lungs, all the way down that hill. *(Aslan and Rudy drop to their knees.)* Getting smaller with every step as the ducks left us behind. *(Rudy breathes heavily in the same rhythm as the wings of the birds. He gently lays his head in Aslan's lap.)*
When we got to the bottom we fell into the grass.
We ate the rest of our onion and fell asleep. *(They are still for a moment.)*
In the morning, we walked back. *(Rudy gets up and leaves.)*

Rudy

(Stopping to say goodbye.) Ýnþallah.

Aslan

Ýnþallah.
For months, Katja would whisper at me as she passed,

Katja

(Crossing the stage behind him.) Coward.

Aslan

And poke me. (*She does.)*

Katja

Coward. *(All exit but Aslan who crosses up and waits.)*

~

Irena

My secret journeys, I took at night, under the covers. My most precious possession as a little girl was my stamp collection. *(She has the stamp album with her.)* I had stamps from all over the world. Not just Eastern Europe and the Soviet Union, but everywhere. My mother and father would bring stamps home from the university. The people in my apartment building would save stamps for me. *(The people of her apartment approach her with gifts.)* My friend, Mariena, lived on the same floor of the apartment building next door. We had a trolley system set up between our windows. Strings on pulleys with a tin can to carry messages and a little bell at each end to ring when a message was ready.

Mariena would collect stamps for me too, put them in the trolley and ring the bell.

(A small bell rings. Mariena enters with a flashlight which is used to light the girls as the stage lights fade out.)

Sometimes, Mariena would stay overnight and we would climb under the covers together with my stamps.

Mariena

Let's go to Japan.

Irena

What do you think it's like?

Mariena

They have tea, and the women wear little pillows on their backs all the time. *(Both girls clasp their hands and bow.)*

Irena

And chopsticks in their hair! *(They giggle and exit: little Japanese girls. Lights up on Aslan.)*

Aslan

Standing on that hilltop with Rudy, straining with all our might toward Chechnya in the imagined distance, I was faced for the first time with the real possibility of belonging. It was like a word on the tip of my tongue. Something almost known that cannot be reached. Understanding is like the ability to fly. The ducks flew on without us. I did not have the knowledge to reach across the short gap between the tips of my fingers and the tips of their wings.

And so I am a translator. Straining constantly into that tantalizing gap. Straining to understand. Caught between one language and another.

I am an action not a thing.

A verb.

And, ironically, until I can learn to fly, there can be no resting place for me.

Irena

Here's a story you've never heard.

When I was ten years old, Kolya was a god. He was the only boy I have ever loved with all the magic of my imagination. Without order or care. Without limit.

We never touched.

My father would sometimes take us, your Uncle Jozef or me, on business trips with him. There I was, on a holiday in Moscow, the capital of all the Soviet Union, at a most impressionable age. Kolya was a blond haired soldier in a crisp uniform, home on leave. So tall.

His little sister ran to him and when he swept her up in his arms I wanted so much to take her place. *(Kolya appears upstage and Anya runs to him. Irena stares with her mouth wide open.)*

Anya
Kolya!

Kolya
Little Anya!

Anya
I'm not little!

Kolya
No, no. You are growing up.

Anya's Mother
Catching flies, Irena? *(Irena's mouth snaps shut.)*

Kolya
Who is this beautiful dark haired young lady?

Irena
Inside I was suddenly warm.

Anya
This is my newest best friend, Irena. She is from Czechoslovakia. *(From Anya's lips, Czechoslovakia sounds like the most mysterious and exciting of places.)* She is staying with us for two whole weeks because her father is here working with Papa.

Kolya
Hello, Irena. *(He speaks in a deliberately provocative baritone. He moves on to embrace his mother. Mother begins to set the table.)*

Irena
I was left with the shape his lips made when he spoke my name.

Kolya was only there for two days and those two days were like a fever. My whole world shimmered in the heat. I watched him out the corner of my eye every chance I got. I looked for his reflection in mirrors, in windows. I could not be caught looking. *(Irena joins the others at the table.)*
I devised elaborate methods to observe him. At meals, I barely touched my food. He sat across the table from me and I found that if I held my spoon just right, he lay in it like a small flame and by tilting it back and forth I could make him come to me and go away again.

Mother
What's wrong, dear? Is it dirty? *(She takes the spoon.)*

Irena
No!
I was almost sure I had been found out. *(All but Kolya exit. Kolya stands half way out looking at her over his shoulder.)*
Two days passed and Kolya left. I did not even see him go. He slipped out of the house early in the morning. He flickered in my dreams.
There was not even a note on my pillow. I checked. *(He smiles slyly and exits.)*
I came home to Bratislava with my father and I soon forgot about Kolya.
But that fall, those two weeks in Moscow.
Boy.

Aslan
Stalin finally died in 1953. I understand it was a long and somewhat painful death. That he was afraid of everyone at the end. That they were also afraid of him. A sick paranoid old man. *(Stalin's aides stand by confused as he*

has a stroke and falls slowly to the floor.)
He had a stroke, an attack, something, while he was alone in his room.
They heard him fall but were afraid to enter. He lay there for hours, helpless and terrified. When they finally broke down the door they found him on the floor, his eyes wide with fear, able only to make buzzing noises. *(He is terrified as they approach him from all sides. He makes buzzing noises through his teeth.)*
It pleases me to think of him like that. Lying in his own shit and making buzzing noises like a bug. *(Aslan joins the aides around Stalin.)*
They say he raised his hand to curse them, but died instead.
(The aides suddenly slap their hands together as though they were killing a fly. Lights out on the tableau. Aslan chuckles.)
So. Stalin died in 1953. Still... it took them three years to pull their heads out of their asses... to began to repair some of the damage.
Even then someone had to go to Moscow and tap Krushchev on the shoulder.

Minister in Charge of the Caucasus
(Crossing to the sleeping Krushchev. He has some trouble waking him.)
Ah-hmm! Comrade Premier. Comrade Premier! *(Krushchev stirs.)* Comrade Premier, there are 2 million people... well less now... illegally deported to Kazakhstan who are waiting to go home to the Caucasus.

Krushchev
Oh, sorry. Go home.

Minister in Charge of the Caucasus
Krushchev says go home.

Aslan

That's good news. How?

Kruschev

(As he exits.) Walk.

Aslan

They had guns.
We walked. *(He walks with the exiles.)*
It was a long way. There was little food. Sometimes we would steal from fields. At least it was summer and there was food to steal.
My sister Katja became very ill. There had been no food for days and my mother was anxious for Katja to eat. One night I went on my own to look for some food.
I found an orchard and was stealing apples when the farmer came out and chased me away.

Farmer

Thief!

Aslan

He beat me with a rake. I had a bad cut on my forehead.
I was not able to hold on any of the fruit.
We went hungry again that night.
(Irena enters upstage and begins to sing, "Dolina", a Russian folk song.)
The next day we met an old man with a little house and garden in the middle of nowhere. Every day he would make a pot of soup to feed the people passing by.

Old Man

Eat. *(He offers the bowl to Katja.)*

Aslan

But for Katja, it was too late.

Katja

No, Aslan, you eat mine.

Aslan

Then she closed her eyes. *(He drinks.)*
It was the most delicious soup I have ever had.
She died that evening.

Old Man

She will sleep in my field. *(The Old Man exits, taking with him whatever piece of clothing or property that identified Katja: a coat or shawl. Katja moves upstage and joins Irena in the song. They continue to sing until the end of the scene.)*

Aslan

You see, there is also kindness everywhere.
(Aslan is joined by his mother.)
It was beautiful. Chechnya. Almost as beautiful as I had imagined.
There was only one problem. *(They turn to face their house where the new owner is sweeping his steps.)* For thirteen years, somebody else had been living in our house. They were Russians.

Mother

Excuse me, this is our house.

Russian

Fuck off.

Mother

But this land is my family's for two hundred years.

Russian

I'll call the army! *(He hurries off.)*

Aslan

Who can blame him. He'd been living there for years.
(He comforts his mother.)
A lot of us slept in the ditch that night. But we had been sleeping in ditches for weeks.
As the sun set, I lay on my back in the grass and looked at the darkening sky.
I was looking for the ducks.
It must have been the wrong season. *(Exits.)*

Irena

I had one stamp. My most special stamp. Mine alone.
It was from France. It was very old.
It had been hand canceled. Someone had written over it in a flowing hand.

French Postal Worker

26 Avril, 1867. Paris. *(She franks the letter and hands it to Irena.)*

Irena

I remember thinking, a hundred years old. Older than Babka.
I don't know where it came from. How it ended up in my collection.
Under my covers at night, I would dream about who sent it. What special message journeyed beneath it. I would become a young French woman reading the letter from her lover.

Lover

(He sweeps in to whisper over her shoulder.)
I will come for you on the morrow.

Irena

I swooned to my pillow. "Amour." *(She whispers, leaning back into her lover and clutching the letter to her heart.)*
It was the only French word I knew besides "Bonjour" and "Oo-la-la." *(The lover exits.)*

There was one more journey I would take by myself. Back to the beach in Bulgaria.
This time, it was sixteen years before, to where my mother met my father after the war.
(Mother and Father. They kneel beside each other, intent on the beach and intensely aware of one another.)
Have I told you this story?
It is the most romantic one I know.
They met on a Monday and didn't speak each other's language.
They communicated by drawing pictures in the sand.
They were married on Friday. *(Mother and father look up at each other and clasp hands.)*
Some nights, I would hold my Bulgarian stamps in my hand and become my mother, falling in love with my father.

Mother and Irena

(Whispering.)
Ja t˘a lubím.

Irena

I would breathe.
And run my fingers over my sheets.
Drawing hearts… and arrows.
(Mother and father kiss.)

Aslan

(Suddenly, interrupting the moment.) My father joined the Chechen Communist Party. *(The mother and Irena exit.)* This may strike you as odd, but as my father put it,

Father

It was Stalin who deported us, Stalin is dead. Krushchev brought us home.

Aslan

They were recruiting heavily all over the Caucasus. There had, understandably, been a
drop in membership over the past thirteen years. My father believed,

Father

It will give my family better opportunities if I am a party member.

Aslan

We had been relocated to Grozny, the capital of Chechnya.

Father

I was an engineer in the oil fields before we left.

Russian Official

We are not hiring Chechens in the oil field.

Aslan

They found him another position for which he had suitable training and experience.

Russian Official

But we need someone to mop floors. *(He hands Father a mop and exits.)*

Aslan

He worked hard. Attended many meetings. *(Father mops his way off the stage.)*

As I have said, he was an optimist.

Schooling was limited for me even here, being the son of a deportee.

We were always criminals. Even now they are still telling lies about us.

Russian One

(Russians One and Two cross the stage gossiping.)

The Chechens were collaborators.

Russian Two

It was better to deport them than leave them to the Nazis. They would only have exterminated them.

Aslan

(Calling after them.) The Nazis never occupied that part of the Caucasus.

Tell the same lie enough times and it becomes the truth. History is made like this.

For me, I was lucky. Next door to us in our apartment in Grozny, was a Swede.*(The Swede enters with a book in his hand.)*

I know what you are thinking, what was a Swede doing in Grozny.

He was a zealot. A communist. A former member of the Swedish Communist Party who had followed his dream and defected to the Soviet Union. He made a meager living teaching Marxism and Scandinavian studies. Me, he didn't get paid for.

But I did things for him. Shopping. Chores. He was an old man.

In exchange he taught me many things. Socialism.

Lindegard

The history of all hitherto existing society is the history of class struggles.

Aslan

Swedish.

Lindegard

Historien om alla hittillsvarande samhällen är historien om klasskamp.

Aslan

A little German.

Lindegard

Die Geschichte aller bisherigen Gesellschaft ist die Geschichte von Klassenkämpfen.

Aslan

I hungered for knowledge and experience. Comrade Lindegard gave me both. (*Comrade Lindegard passes the book to Aslan and stands next to him looking out over the city.)*

I devoured the books in his library. I swallowed his teachings whole. We often wandered the streets of Grozny together and I ate the city too.

Lindegard

The river *(he points it out)*

Aslan

for breakfast.

Lindegard

The old mansions of the British oil barons

Aslan

for lunch.

Lindegard

The university

Aslan

for dinner.
I was insatiable. It was as though a vacuum had been created in me all those years in Kazakhstan which must be filled.
He was a kind man. *(Lindegard lays his hand briefly on Aslan's shoulder and then retreats to a chair where he seems to sleep.)* The first I had known beyond my family. I too became a zealot.
As only teenagers can.
As only the hungry eat.
As only one who is loved for the first time, loves.
I loved that old man.

Then one morning, just before my eigthteenth birthday, I entered his apartment to find him ...dead ...across his desk.
He had laid his head forward as though to rest.
His spectacles had fallen off.
Beside his right hand was a pen.
He had been underlining passages from a book. *(Aslan slips the book from the grasp of the dead man.)*
The book was Lenin's "The State and Revolution."
The passage he had underlined was this *(He passes the book to Lenin who strikes his famous pose, book clasped to chest and arm raised.)*

Lenin

We set ourselves the ultimate aim of abolishing the state; abolishing all organized and systematic violence, all use of violence against man in general.

Aslan

(Pause) I joined the army.

(He exits. Lights fade to black and music begins: a haunting lyrical ballad perhaps, a dance.)

Part Three: Invasion

Irena

(Entering in her nightgown.)

From the time that I was a little girl, I believed that I could see the light.

The pools of light that surround us as we move through the world like lanterns.

Not everyday.

Not every time I tried.

Sometimes only in dreams.

Less and less as I got older.

I could especially see the lights of my family, my friends.

As though love clarifies the vision.

(Mother and Father have entered with candles. They kiss Irena on the cheek and depart.)

Sometimes at night, after the electric lights wereswitched off and my mother and father were slipping out the door, I looked with eyes half seeing through dreams, and they were candles whose light followed them out, all in a rush to get through the door before it closed. But whose warmth lingered in the room and settled upon me.

(The candles are transferred to a candelabra that lifts above the stage and upstage the parents and their guests laugh and talk. We cannot hear them.)

In the spring of 1968, I was too young to understand the political events unfolding around me, but I had other perceptions, another set of eyes, like baby teeth.

When people are happy, hopeful, in love, their lights are brighter. They give the impression of glowing. Of lifting.

Floating over the earth.
Walking on air.
Lifting to the sky. To hang among the stars. Like lanterns.
In the spring of 1968, it was as though the whole of the city was lifted up into the air and went drifting lazily out over the fields of Slovakia. Apple orchards, from above, like snowfields, white with blossoms.
Light shone from the darkest corners and for a time we were all creatures of the air rather than the earth.
I saw it most in my mother and father. They floated like lovers on a cushion of air. Like something of their first weeks together had been reawakened.
It was infectious. Guests giggled over dinner. Talked of the brave new words appearing in the papers daily. Words people had only dared speak in the dark, that now walked the streets like citizens.

Dinner Guest
Raising his glass.
Svoboda!

Irena
I felt taller. Swollen with light Lighter than air. That I could have flown with the pigeons that roosted on the ledge outside my window. *(The parents and guests fade to black.)*

I had a dream one night.
I floated up out of my bed. Floated out through my open window into the air above the street.
Below me there were lights in the trees along the boulevard like Christmas.
I turned to see my friend Mariena float out of her window.
(Mariena enters in a long nightgown.)
She wore a long gown that hid her feet and trailed behind her like water.

I wore the same gown.
She came to me, I took her hand, and together we flew about the city. *(They do.)*
Over rooftops. Parks.
We chased each other through the trees.
Laughing.
All around us were others. *(The citizens emerge in their nightgowns to dance about the city.)*
The citizens of Bratislava in their nightgowns
dancing in the warm night air
lanterns
up among the blossoms in the square
while the city looked on in approval
through the warm yellow eyes
of the buildings
around us.
(There is dancing.)

Aslan

The Prague Spring.
(Behind him the citizens continue to dance.)
Communism with a human face.
It began in January. New leaders replaced old ones accused of corruption. Censorship was lifted. Reforms swept the country. Dubcek as party secretary. Svoboda as premier.
In Czech, Svoboda means freedom.

Citizens

Svoboda! *(The citizens freeze.)*

Irena

When he became a teacher, your father cut his hair. I would reach up to touch the back of his neck but there was nothing there anymore but stubble. I guess it made a better impression in the classroom. *(All exit but Aslan.)*

Aslan

Of course, in the army, we were not allowed to hear this. Our ears belonged to Brezhnev. From Moscow, we heard only the grumblings of the restless bear.

By this time, I was a communications officer in the Motor Rifle Division of the 38th Army. Tanks. I spoke six languages and had been learning Czech and Slovak since early in the year. In the modern communist march to a new and glorious internationalism, it had become desirable to mix up the nationalities of our great soviet confederation. As a result, in my unit, about one man in ten spoke Russian. The other nine spoke nine other languages.

One of my jobs was to translate orders to the soldiers.

Russian Officer

Moy ati tanki! *(Get those tanks washed!)*

Aslan

Da!

(Translates the order into Hungarian for a passing soldier.)

Mosd meg a tankot! *(Wash the tanks.)*

Soldier

Mi? *(What?)*

Aslan

Mosd...meg...a...tan...kot.

Soldier Off

Meny a francba! *(Go to hell.)*

Aslan

This is hell!

Nobody knew what was going on from one minute to the next.

In the midst of this confusion, there was Kolya. The perfect soldier. *(Kolya enters. He brings shovels and they dig together as Aslan speaks.)* The kind of young man that is on the posters. A hero for the people. I enjoyed him very much. He was polite, intelligent, hard working, and more than a little naïve.

One time, when we were cleaning the latrine, even then he was extolling the virtues of communism.

Comrade, when we have true communism, when we are all equal, all encouraged, expected to pursue our true paths in the great march toward the common good, who then will shovel the shit? *(Aslan dumps a shovel full of shit on Kolya's boot.)*

Kolya

(He shakes off his boot and deliberately reciprocates.)

We will take turns. We will each accept with honor our responsibility for the good of all. *(He bows like a dancer and Aslan laughs. Kolya exits.)*

Aslan

Kolya reminded me of the strong convictions I had carried into the army. But the experiences of the last eight years had brought me to a more... temperate view. He was unshakable. That was both a strength and, perhaps, a fatal flaw.

In May and June we had been engaged in military exercises in Czechoslovakia. Mostly in the east, the Carpathian Mountains. When they ended, we withdrew into the Ukraine and stopped just across the border. Made camp inside the fringes of the forest where we could not be seen from the air. There we began a general

mobilization. In the Soviet army, this was a kind of a spreading cancer. *(Mobilization. Troop movements begin. Marching. Soldiers gather upstage in preparation.)*
Reservists, farmers and laborers mostly, who had not seen action or training for ten years, were called up. Units that had operated with reduced personnel were filled. Four men in a tank that had only held a driver. Then the units were split in two and more reservists were called up. New troops in old uniforms arriving daily in the broken down and patched together vehicles that served as grocery vans or farm trucks during peace time.
We waited there for months. Life developed a growing and incessant rhythm of anticipation.
Our tanks crouching under their camouflage nets.
Pacing to the edge of the wood and back five six times a day.
Polishing our weapons.
Polishing our shoes.
Officers worried about morale.
Farmers worried about their crops. *(A tableau has been built over the past few lines. Aslan moves to join them.)*

At nightfall
as the light seeped into the damp earth
Into the loam like centuries
The trees, the leaves, the tanks
our comrades, our shining faith
grew less and less distinct
until they were just shades
and the sound of men breathing
taking in air
and releasing it
seventeen thousand times a day.
(Everyone breathes in unison as lights fade on the tableau. Two long full breaths.)

I had no doubt that we would invade. It was only a matter of timing.

Irena

My mother was away to England for another teaching conference. My father was busy most of the day at the university for his research or preparing his classes for the fall. It was early August. My brother and I had the house to our selves. And we did what any children would do in a similar circumstance. We broke all of the rules and made an incredible mess. My father would yell at us when he came home and make us clean up but the next day we would do it again.

We had a balcony that looked over the wide boulevard in front of our apartment. *(Jozef builds the balcony with chairs while Irena speaks.)* The boulevard led to the square in the center of the city. The sidewalks below our balcony were always busy. Full of people walking. Imagine the possibilities for two wild children perched like eagles on our ledge five stories above a crowded street.

Jozef

Ty mas smiesnu hlavu! *(You have a funny head!)*

Irena

We threw water. We spit. *(Jozef runs to get a knickknack and string.)*
Our favorite game though was to take knickknacks from inside the apartment, tie strings to them and dangle them off the balcony to tease the passers-by. We would lower them to hang at eye level, to catch their attention, and then, when they reached for them, we would yank them up out of the way.

We could play this game for hours. Fishing for Slovaks.
(Jozef does this.)
The more valuable the object at the end of the string, the more delicious the thrill.
That afternoon, we tied our string around the neck of my mother's precious crystal dove and dangled it over the concrete sidewalk five stories below. It was the best.
And then to our horror, someone grabbed it. *(A passer-by.)*
And wouldn't let go. It suddenly wasn't funny anymore.

Jozef
Irena!

Irena
Please! Please let go! My mother will kill us! Please!

Couple on the Street
Please let go! My mother will kill us!

Irena
And then,

Mother
Čo to robit˘e?! *(What's going on?)*

Irena
There, at the bus stop, was my mother, back from England.
(Lights fade on the memories.)
I remember several days of no desserts and early bedtimes. My parents laughter from the living room as I lay in the dark and pondered where they had hidden the string.

Aslan
When the time finally came, our political officer stood on

a box labeled "Made in the USA" and read to us a letter from some Czech labor group.

Political Officer

Listen what they write to us! "You must rescue us from the imperialists who are subverting our country." My comrades! If the infection is allowed to take hold in that country, it will spread like wildfire throughout the Warsaw Pact and our nations will fall to it like dominoes.

Aslan

A popular idea in the sixties.

Political Officer

My comrades! We will make a glorious stand for the new world, for communism, and for brotherhood! *(There are cheers. He passes out buckets of paint.)*

Aslan

Then we were issued white paint to make rings around the tops of our vehicles. To distinguish them from the enemy. *(The stage clears and the lights dim.)*

And that night, under cover of darkness, we shook ourselves, left our forest lairs, and with our still wet paint glistening in the starlight, we crossed the border and fell like snow on the sleeping Slovaks.

Irena

(Sound: The roar of tanks on cobble stones.) I woke up in the middle of the night to a roar that made my windows clatter. "Mami! Tato!"

Father

Here Irena. Come to the balcony.

Irena

Thundering by on the cobblestones where summer had wandered on a warm and aimless evening only hours before, were hundreds of tanks.
What is it, Mami?

Mother

Maybe it is an exercise. Military maneuvers.

Father

It can't be maneuvers. Not in the city. Not in the middle of the night.

Irena

My mother turned white even in the light of the moon.

Mother

Oh, my God. Oh, my God. It is an invasion. They are invading us. In England, people at the conference said there would be an invasion. I told them no, they would not dare.
I told them no.

Irena

Below us, the line of tanks continued to pass. And with every one, the lights from the balconies and windows around me dimmed a little and another part of the city dropped back to earth with an audible thud.
(The family tableau breaks up. The actors slowly whirling the chairs in confused circles about the stage. Aslan enters into the middle of this.)

Aslan

There was no armed resistance. There was no one to fight against. We came roaring in, there was no one there, and our momentum was carrying us in dizzying meaningless circles. We were in danger of losing our footing altogether. Very many soldiers did not even know what country we were in. Many thought the great liberation of Europe had started. In Bratislava, they had removed all the street signs. It happened overnight. Replaced them with new ones that all said Dubcek.

Citizens

(The whirling suddenly stopped. The chairs hit the floor.) Dubcék!

Irena

All the numbers disappeared off the apartments and houses. I remember seeing Mr. Chočena on the street the next day.
Mr. Chočena, Mr. Chočena, how do you know where to take the mail?

Mr. Chočena

We know very well where we are young lady. It is only the Russians who are lost.

Mother

(Mother gathers her family around her.) There will be a shortage of food and supplies. We must get to the stores before everything is gone. Irena, go to the store in the square.

Irena

The Russians were there before me. *(She exits.)*

Aslan

People crowded the streets to yell at us. *(Kolya stands with him facing upstage into the taunts of the crowd.)*

Citizens

How can you do this? How can you live with yourselves? *(They spit and shake their fists.)*

Pigs! Get out! We don't want you here!

Aslan

They wrote on the walls.

A Citizen

Ivan, go home! Your girlfriend is fucking your brother!

Aslan

If my fellow soldiers could not understand the words, they could certainly understand the gestures, the rotten vegetables, the stones.

The strongest, most committed Communists amongst us faltered. *(Aslan stares at Kolya and the young soldier turns, his face showing his fear and confusion.)*

Citizens

(*Chanting.*) Dubćek. Dubćek. Dubćek. (*And then changing to.*) Svo bo da. Svo bo da. *(The chanting continues.)*

Aslan

It will be better if we ignore them. They will grow tired of their yelling and move on. Leave us alone.

Kolya

We must reach out to these people. They are under the spell of the imperialists. We must educate them about their danger. We must engage them. Illuminate them. It is part of our mission.

Citizens

Go home! Go home! Go home! Go home! Go home!

(The chanting carries on over the next speech. Irena joins the crowd.)

Kolya

You must resist the imperialism of the West! *(Kolya is cut off from Aslan and hounded by the crowd.)*

Citizens

Go home!

Kolya

We were invited by your own people! We have a letter!

Citizens

Get out! Go home!

Kolya

We are your brothers! We would not abandon you!

Citizen

We don't want you!

Aslan

(Drawing the crowds attention away from Kolya.) We were invited!

Citizen

Who invited you?

Aslan

Members of your own government!

Citizens

Name them! Who?

Aslan

I will show you the letter!

Citizens

Go home! Go home! Go home! *(Carries on over Aslan's next speech.)*

Aslan

I was ashamed in the face of their constant unwavering commitment and yet I began to grow into my part like an actor. The more they argued, the stronger my performance. It was like the thrill of battle and my words were blades sparking against theirs. Back and forth we parried across the square, my sword against fifty.

The crowd noise fades away and all chorus movement ceases or continues in slow pantomime.

Irena

That is when I saw him. Kolya. And the crowd faded away. He was standing by the tank with a rifle in his hands. I almost didn't recognize him. So unlike the crisp confident young soldier of Moscow. His face was covered with stubble. He wore a worn, oil-stained coverall. But it was him and the fever that had held me a year before returned. Strange and unwelcome here on my own streets, like the invading army in our midst.

I stood swaying between fear and desire.

Between the soldier and the summer trees that lined the boulevard.

I walked up to the tank.

Kolya?

He did not hear me. He was staring at the crowd as though they were an approaching tidal wave about to wash over him.

(The crowd noise swells again. She must raise her voice to be heard.)
His eyes were wild. Lost.
Kolya! It is Irena! KOLYA!!
(Suddenly aware, he turns and points his rifle at Irena. She screams.)

(All sound and movement ceases.)

Aslan
A high shrill scream stopped us all.

Irena
The crowd stopped.

Aslan
We turned to look in the direction of the tank.

Irena
I could not hear it anymore.

Aslan
At Kolya with his rifle leveled against a small girl.

Irena
Only the rustling of the leaves behind me.

Aslan
It was like a movie.

Irena
I saw the recognition cross his face.

Aslan
The rising scream of the young girl.

Irena
And then a horrible shame.

Aslan
The retreating distance between us.

Irena
From the corner of my eye,

Aslan
Our legs frozen to the paving stones.

Irena
I could see my brother moving toward me.

Aslan
That one young man running.

Irena
I watched the rifle swing away.

Black out.
The sound of a rifle shot.

Intermission

ACT TWO

Part Three: Invasion (continued)

(The act opens with the swelling of the same crowd noise we heard at the end of Act One. A young girl's scream into the darkness ends the noise.)

Aslan
A high shrill scream stopped us all.

Irena
The crowd stopped.

Aslan
We all turned to look in the direction of the tank.

Irena
I could not hear it anymore.

Aslan
At Kolya with his rifle leveled against a small girl.

Irena
Only the rustling of the leaves behind me.

Aslan
It was like a movie.

Irena
I could see the look of recognition cross his face.

Aslan
The rising scream of the young girl.

Irena
And then a horrible shame.

Aslan
The retreating distance between us.

Irena
From the corner of my eye,

Aslan
Our legs frozen to the paving stones.

Irena
I could see my brother moving toward me.

Aslan
That one young man running.

Irena
I watched the rifle swing away.

Aslan
Kolya swung the rifle around and took it into his mouth.

Irena
The lips that had spoken my name open to receive it.

Aslan
The explosion of the gun. *(There is no shot this time.)*

Irena
I don't remember a sound.

Aslan
The blonde head.

Irena
Only the explosion of red.

Aslan
The promise of communism.

Irena
In the air.

Aslan
Bursting.

Irena
A thousand apples falling to the ground.

Aslan
His body flopping forward. A final bow.
(Kolya bows, presents his rifle to Aslan and exits.)

Irena
From the ground, over my brother's shoulder, as he asked if I was alright, I could see the blue sky and the leaves dancing in a light summer breeze.

Aslan
All of our words. *(He exits.)*

Irena
Yes, Jozef. I am fine.

Part Four: Departures

Irena

With that shot, all the lights went out. In the days that followed, I do not remember panic, grief, even fear about what I had witnessed in the square. It was almost something that had happened to another little girl, as though I stood outside it.

Almost as though I began in that moment. That I came in to the world as a blank page, was given the knowledge, like a script, of what my life before had been.

Suddenly everything was solidly and undeniably real.

(pause)

About a month later my mother received an invitation to a wedding in England. A university student had stayed with us in the summer and she invited us all to the wedding. In the first few weeks after the invasion, before the Russians took over the border posts, it was easier to leave the country. The government was issuing exit visas on the slightest of pretexts. Our names were all on the invitation and my parents were able to obtain permission for us to go. My mother left a week early to help the bride get ready.

Two days before we left to join her, my father sat us down at the table.

Father

We will not be coming back.

Jozef

What do you mean, we will not be coming back.

Father

We are leaving Czechoslovakia for ever.

Irena

Preco musime ist? Ja sa bojim, Tato. Je chcem ostat doma. *(Why do we have to go? I'm afraid Tato. I want to stay home.)*

Father

I know you are afraid, Irena, but you can't stay home. We have to go. Your mother and I lived through the madness of Stalin. We will not sit by and let our children grow up in that kind of paranoia. Everyone afraid of each other. We will be leaving in two days. You can tell no one. We do not know who to trust.

Jozef

But the wedding. Mother.

Father

The wedding is a hoax to get us out of the country. Your mother went ahead to make preparations for our arrival in England. She did not want you to be in a refugee camp in Austria.

Irena

What if she is caught?

Father

She said she would send a telegram. There would be a message hidden in it for us. If she had problems, it would be raining in England. If things were OK, the weather would be fine. This arrived today. *(He passes a telegram to the children.)*

Mother

Bride excited stop miss you all stop see you in a couple of days stop it is a glorious autumn in England stop

Irena

My departure from Czechoslovakia did not begin with leaving the country, it began with the knowledge that I was going and that I could tell no one.
From that moment, I was different. Separated from my friends, my classmates, the whole city, by that one simple fact.
The next day, my last at school, my mouth was filled with a farewell I could not speak. I sat silent through the whole day. Avoided friends. Walked home alone.
That evening, my father told us,

Father

You can take nothing but one suitcase of clothing. No games, no toys, nothing that will arouse the slightest suspicion at the border. Getting caught could mean anything. Prison, exile. Our family broken up. Do you understand?
We are not coming back.

Irena

Later, as I packed and re-packed my clothes, leaving this, taking that, everything I saw, I saw for the last time. I walked around the apartment touching things.
My piano the colour of cream.
The golden tassels from a lamp shade.
An empty spoon.
Feeling for memories already false and fading.

(Her brother hands Irena her stamps and she clutches them to her.)
I held my stamp collection for a very long time. I slept with it beside my bed. But no journeys filled my head except this last one that lay before me like a dark sea. In the morning, my father checked all of our things. *(He does.)* Declared us safe.

Father
OK.

Irena
When he left, I quickly stuffed my stamps beneath the skirts in my bag. *(She does this.)* Then I wrote a note for Mariena and left it in the trolley for her to find. *(She gives a note to Mariena. A small bell rings.)*

Mariena
(She reads.)
"Dovidenia."
(And then looks up.)

Irena
Goodbye. *(Their hands are raised as though in a mirror.)*

(At the train station. Aslan and another soldier are checking the papers of travelers. They do this while he speaks. The travelers reacting silently to his gestures.)

Aslan
It was hot that day. Late September. I remember my uniform sticking to my back like another skin that I couldn't shed.

Over the weeks I had gone from guarding a post office to patrolling the streets to searching baggage at the train station. A position for which I was possibly better suited because of my languages.

All day long we had been processing tourists.

Businessmen. Travelers. Some from

Bratislava going away. Some from other places going home. Slovakia. Prague. Bohemia. Hungary. Austrians from the west. An English reporter. We detained and searched him. Not because we suspected him of anything, but because he was from England and we could. Sometimes we would stop people and search them just to have a break from the monotony. *(A man enters. As Aslan speaks and checks the man's papers, the soldier searches his bag.)*

Sometimes because we did not like the way they looked. Maybe their shirt did not fit right or was the wrong color.

The old guy. Make him sweat.

The beautiful woman. *(They tip their hats and let the woman pass. They stare after her. Then Aslan to the soldier.)*

I don't care if she is an American spy. She has exquisite breasts.

Soldier

On second thought, let's bring her in, maybe she is concealing a weapon. *(They laugh.)*

Aslan

Give hot bored soldiers some power and see what happens.

We feed off each other's boredom. Give ourselves permission to be just a little crazy.

Irena

(Entering with her father.)

My father approached the counter and put our bags on it.

Aslan

Papers. *(Father hands them over.)*
I remember them. A man and his children. They had tickets for Vienna. Their exit visas said London.
What is your business in London?

Father

I am a professor of engineering and a member of the Academy of Science. I am going to the wedding of a family friend.

Aslan

These are your children?

Father

Yes.

Aslan

Are they also members of the Academy of Science?

Father

Of course not. *(Irena takes her father's hand.)* She has also invited them. See, I have the invitation.

Aslan

Where is their mother?

Father

She has gone ahead to help with the preparations.

Aslan

Is that true? *(This is spoken directly at Irena. It is the only moment in the play when their eyes meet.)*

Irena

Yes…

Aslan

The man was calm but his daughter was nervous.

Soldier

(The soldier had opened Irena's bag and was rummaging through it. He holds up the stamp collection.)
What is this? *(He passes it to Aslan.)*

Father

That is my daughter's stamp collection.

Aslan

Why is she taking her stamps to London?
Nobody takes a stamp collection on a holiday.

Father

I...she takes it everywhere.
(There is a pause. Aslan stares at the father and then speaks very slowly and carefully.)

Aslan

I think you are not planning to come back.

Father

That is not true. We are just going for the wedding. Look, I have only two hundred British pounds.
(He holds out his wallet. No one looks at it. The soldier beside the table raises his rifle.)

Irena

My father's hand felt very cold. It was shaking. I remember the shaking. Almost imperceptible. *(She begins to cry.)*

Aslan

I knew they were defecting. There could be no doubt.
In that moment, holding that little girl's stamp collection in my hand, I had such power over their lives. I could destroy them with a word. The soldier next to me, he knew it. He was raising his gun. We were going to arrest them.
And then... there was something about the girl's eyes. Something that reminded me of my sister, Katja. She was about this girl's age that night on the road to Chechnya

Time is so relative.
Sometimes it is quick. Sometimes slow.
That day it folded itself like a map.
(To the father.)
Your children will be late starting in their new school. Go.
(Father gathers the bags quickly and they walk out toward the waiting train.)

Aslan

Stop!
(Irena and her father turn and look back.)
They will check your bags again at the border.
(The other soldier cannot believe his ears.)
I gave them back the stamps. I let them go to London.

Aslan

I did not even try to explain. I looked up at the faces of the people around me. Trying to leave a country that I was in the process of destroying. Crushing a hope that had been growing all spring like apples. Cutting the trees. The fruit spoiling on the ground.
All around me people starving for a single bite.

Irena

On the train my father did not say anything to me. He sat with his head down and he held my hand. My stamp collection sat on his lap.

On the way to the border from Bratislava is a tunnel.

When we entered the tunnel my father stood up very quickly and opened the window in our compartment. Then he threw my stamp collection out into the darkness. *(It flies up and disappears overhead into the darkness. Irena struggles to stop him but he wraps her up in his arms and holds her very tight.)*

Tato, no!

My father held me very close.

I was angry. I did not see the tears in his eyes until months after.

We did not have any trouble at the border.

We spent one night in Vienna with friends.

When we stepped off the train in London where my mother was waiting, it was raining.

(Stamps begin to flutter down from above. The chorus is revealed upstage swaying slightly in the near darkness.)

Sometimes I can see the stamps fluttering down into the blackness like leaves.

They glow a little. They slip back and forth as they settle toward the tracks.

As the train passes, they are caught in the slipstream and briefly, they chase us, reluctant to part. *{The chorus reach out for her, then disappear into the darkness)*

Sometimes I am standing at the back of the train and I can step off and join them and we rush along in the empty darkness after the silent locomotive that disappears down the tunnel.

And sometimes out of the distance I hear my own small voice calling, No Tato.

No.

(The stamps turn to snow.)

Aslan and Yevgeny enter in uniform, marching, to take positions at the gate.

Aslan

It was a cold day in Hell. An English expression I like.

Do you know the story of Orpheus and Eurydice? *(The soldier listens.)*
Orpheus loved her but on their wedding day she was bitten by a snake and died. He could not live without her so he descended into Hell to retrieve her from the kingdom of the dead. Because Orpheus could sing so beautifully, Hades made a bargain with him. She was allowed to follow him out but, on the way, he could not look back to see if she was there or he would lose her forever. It was a long way and his desire was too great. As they neared the exit from the underworld, he could no longer resist. He looked back and ...psht...she was gone. When he emerged into the living world, alone, he was torn to pieces by the Furies.
His mistake was that he could not let go of his past.

I remember his name...Yevgeny. The young soldier serving with me that day. The Russians had tightened security and I had moved all the way across Czechoslovakia to the West German border. For two weeks I stood in the cold February air and checked papers. Searched vehicles. Baggage. Passed on or turned back face after anonymous face. The faces, the papers were the same. I could not see beyond them. *(A woman crosses. Her papers are not in order and the soldier bustles her off.)*
If they protested when I turned them back, I could not hear it.

A kind of flat despair had settled on me that reflected the weather.

Everyday I was simply coldly efficient.

Everyday I was a simply a Soviet soldier. *(Yevgeny returns to his post.)*

Yevgeny was, I think, somewhat in awe of me. He was fresh out of training and saw me as some kind of role model. *(A salute.)* A battle hardened and dedicated socialist warrior. I wore the role like a straight jacket.

(A pause as he remembers, a hand in the air.)

That day was the same. A little bit colder maybe. A little bit darker.

(A man enters and moves to the border post.) The man was no different than twenty others who had crossed before him. He was a German. He wore a leather coat. He carried a small bag. His papers were in order. I motioned to Yevgeny to lift the gate and watched him step past me into the fifty yards of no man's land that led to the West Germans on the other side.

Yevgeny

You did not check his bag.

Aslan

What?

Yevgeny

You did not check his bag. There may have been things in his bag. It should be checked, shouldn't it?

Aslan

I stared after him... and possibility filled me like breath. As though I had been drowning and had not known it until this moment.

You are right, Yevgeny. I should have checked his bag. I will go after him.

Yevgeny

You can not cross into German territory. He has gone too far.

Aslan

I will get him. Hold this. *(He passes his rifle, ducked under the gate and steps out after the German.)*
Fifty yards.

Yevgeny

Wait!

Aslan

The German looked over his shoulder and quickened his pace.
I could not run.
My eyes reached after him like hands.
I moved ahead of myself.
The snow not falling hard enough to obliterate my footsteps.
The West Germans with their weapons trained on me as the man reached the border.
With twenty yards to go, I raised my hands, empty, above my head.
There could no longer be any doubt that I was defecting.
Yevgeny behind me holding my rifle. *(Yevgeny has his rifle pointed at Aslan but cannot bring himself to fire.)* The skin of my back already curling as if around the bullet.

Yevgeny

Please!

Aslan

As I crossed those fifty yards, I shed my past like a skin. I burst out of it and it fell behind me... a dead thing.
(Yevgeny withdraws. Aslan is alone on stage. He sheds his

great coat like a skin.)

I... would... not... look... back.

(He begins to sing, softly at first but growing in intensity as he starts dancing to his own song. The song is in Russian and the following is a phonetic transcription.)

Ya nyeh Sovietski	*I am not a Soviet*
Ya tolka Russki	*I am simply a Russian*
Ya Peterburski anarchiste	*I am a Peterburg anarchist*
Menya zanyali	*They arrested me*
Na Siber dali	*Took me to Siberia*
Padomu shto na communiste	*Because I'm not a communist*

(He repeats the tune with meaningless sounds, nyah nyah nyah nyah nyah, as the dance builds in intensity and becomes a kind of purging, a shriving. He finishes released, exhausted.)
Besides, with his shapeless overcoat and bad complexion, Yevgeny would not be the kind of lover I would like to have following me out of Hell.

~

Irena
We came to Canada because Australia was too far away.
We came to Toronto because it had opera.
We had nothing. The Canadian consulate in London lent us the money for airline tickets and arranged for our flights. All we had to do was pass the physical examinations and pick a place to go. *(Mother consults with an official while Irena gets a physical.)*

Mother

Where is a city with a university?

Official

(Pointing to Edmonton on the map.) Edmonton.

Mother

Oh! Too far north. Too cold. *(She runs her finger slowly across the map and stops.)* Win-nee-peg.

Official

(*laughing*) Colder than Edmonton. Colder than hell.

Mother

Where is there an opera house? Where is culture?

Doctor

Send them to Toronto. *(Mother, the official and the doctor exit.)*

Irena

So we came to Toronto.
For almost a year we lived in a one bedroom apartment with only three things.
In the bedroom were mattresses side by side on the floor on which all four of us slept.
In the closet we had a vacuum cleaner because my mother insisted. *(She crosses with a vacuum cleaner in her arms.)*
In the dining room we had a picnic table.

Father

(Proudly pointing off at the picnic table.)
One day it will sit in the backyard of our new Canadian home.

Irena

Later, because we could not afford to go to the opera, my mother bought a record player.

Mother

(Crossing with a record player.)
I do not want you to grow up uncultured.

Irena

(Irena remembers the music. Hums a bar and stops in mid-phrase.)
It is the first day in my new school in Ontario, and I do not speak a word of English.
I sat in the strange classroom and tried so hard to understand what was going on that I got a headache.
Everyday for weeks I came home with a headache.
They pulled me out of class a half hour a day to teach me English but that first day I couldn't speak a word.
They put me a grade ahead because the schools in Bratislava were more advanced.
I was younger than the other girls. *(The girls stare at her.)*
I looked foreign.
I wore strange clothes.
I could not speak the language.
That afternoon, walking home, I could not understand the words they called after me but their intentions entered my back like knives.

Girl

Pig!

Irena

Killed the last remnants of the little Slovakian girl who saw people as pools of light.

Who, under the covers with her stamps, dreamed secret journeys in the night.
This journey that I had begun was too real to be mistaken for a dream.
I learned quickly.

Aslan

(Aslan and Inge in step, almost dancing. Intense but not touching. Suggestion perhaps of an apache.)
I met your mother on the docks of Stockholm. *{They move apart.)*
Swedish was the only western language I knew so it is where I went.
I ended up on the docks because I could smell the sea. I could taste it, spit into it.
At night I could stand at the edge of it and feel its hands on me. Like fingers whispering to my skin in the little voices of quick waves lapping at the pilings. As though the water held something for me.
A promise ... of place.

She worked in the dispatcher's office.
I worked loading ships alongside men from all over the world. *(Men cross the stage carrying crates. They call to each other in several languages.)* We spoke among us a strange mixture of languages that somehow communicated everything we needed to know. It was like the old man's delicious soup. It fed us all.
Your mother knew how glorious she was. The desire we all carried for her...like cargo.
She was a very confident young woman. *(The men flirt with her. She laughs but does not accompany them. She has her eye on Aslan.)*

Everyone flirted with her. She flirted back. She would join us sometimes for a drink but she would not go out with any one man. She always left early. Alone.
I don't know what made her look at me any differently.
My languages?
The books I was always reading?
One day in April, she noticed a battered copy of Rilke's poems I had in my back pocket.

Inge

(She snatches the book from his pocket, flips it open at random and reads.)

"We don't accomplish our love in a single year,
as the flowers do;
the timeless blood of ancient trees flows through
our arms when we love."

Aslan

I think they were the first words we exchanged. *(She looks up at him astonished and then exits with his book.)*
I was not the only worker on the docks who read poetry but, luckily, I was the only one with Rilke in my pocket that day.
(He pauses and moves down stage as Inge exits.)
There was a half moon the night you were born.
I stood outside the hospital and watched it slip from the clouds long enough for a breath and then back under.
I remember how my own breath followed it, out...and in.
Gasping. While, inside, you, too, were gasping for life.
I remember the taste of salt.
You were... beautiful, my... *(There is a long pause here. He has not said these words for thirty years.)*... my son.
I named you for my brother. Illya.

Irena

Life became ordered. I learned to speak English. I finished

school and went to university.
I met your father there and fell in love. He graduated and went west. When I graduated, I did not know what to do so I went west too. I found him and we got married.
(Tableau: Married. She adjusts his suit collar.) That damn suit.
We had children. Beautiful children, my girl.
When I was first pregnant, sometimes he would lay his head on my belly.

Husband

Don't. I'm listening.

Aslan

In the months after, something... for me... changed. More and more I could not be in the house. I took more shifts. I walked often to the sea. *(He speaks these next lines to Inge.)*
We need more money. I have to work more. I can't make enough on the docks.
(Discovering this as he speaks) It was a lie. I was afraid of her. Of you. Everything I had ever cared for had been ripped away or left behind. The more I loved you, the more afraid I became.

Irena

I became a teacher of language, just like my mother and her mother before her. And your father is a teacher. We always knew what we were doing from week to week. From year to year. There were no questions. No risks. Eighteen years have gone by.
You must understand. They were not bad years. I would not change them. I do not regret them or you. Oh my girl, never you. You are closer to me than you will know until you have your own daughter. *(Irena and her husband exit.)*

Aslan

An Italian friend of mine got me a job on a freighter going to the Mediterranean. It was a little more money. That was my excuse.

You were both at the docks the day I sailed. *(He takes the baby briefly from Inge.)*

I held you in my arms, Illya. I kissed you both goodbye. *(There is no kiss between the lovers; just longing and remembrance as Aslan hands the baby back.)*

I swear I did not know ... I was not coming back. *(Inge hands him back his book of Rilke's poems and slips into the background.)*

I think Inge did. She stayed and watched the ship move out of the harbour for a very long time.

So... we sailed to the Mediterranean. Every time we were paid, I sent money to Inge. Every port we stopped in I sent something for you. Little toys, flags, postcards.

Did you get them?

No, of course...you were too young to remember.

I didn't go back to visit.

One day, about a year later, the money I sent came back with a note.

Inge

We don't want your money. *(She turns and exits.)*

Aslan

I had no words.

Do you know? I can make love in thirteen languages but I still do not know what it is.

I think to love one must stop. *(He makes a fist.)* And then open like a flower.

(Opens fist, palm up, slowly and fully, then snaps it shut.)

I could not do it.

Part Five: Endings

Chorus

Through all the years of our lives, our stories weave together and our stories unravel and the patterns are not really so unusual after all.
Listen now while we bring our tales to a close.

Aslan

All these languages. I have twelve now. I think? Twelve? The languages have been a passport for me. For a time, I moved back and forth across the face of Europe translating for business. Government. To make a living. All the time looking for something. A place. A word.
Once, for a little publishing house in England, I did some translations of Rilke. *(He holds the book close to his heart.)* To make a life.
When the protests started in Prague in 1989, when the neat seams of logic began to come apart, I was able to reenter the country. I stood in the square with two hundred thousand Czechoslovakians and we sang down the government by candlelight. That is life.*(The citizens enter with candles. One is given to each of the other actors on stage, including Aslan.)*

Irena

When I was a child, I could see the magic. The light.
I hope, with all of this... this separation... leaving... I hope you still can.
But my vision has been obscured for a long time.
I had forgotten.

And then things began to change

Citizens

(They sing the first few bars of the Czechoslovakian national anthem and then begin to chant.)
Kde domov muj, kde domov muj? *(Where is my home? Where is my home?)*

Irena

We had been married about nine years.
I was doing the dishes when I heard the chanting.

Citizens

(A low steady rhythmical chant.)
Svo bo da. Svo bo da. Svo bo da. Svo bo da. *(etc.)*

Irena

It was just after eleven o'clock, November 17, 1989.
You are in bed. You are only five.
I put the cloth down beside the sink and move into the dining room. It's dark. Your father is sitting in his chair watching the news. He seems to flicker in the light of the television. It is Czechoslovakia. Wenceslas Square. The announcer says it started as a student demonstration. Every night the crowds grew and grew. Tonight, there are hundreds of thousands standing in the square.
Vaclav Havel addresses the crowd. *(The citizens pause and listen.)*

Vaclav Havel

We shall never give up our ideals, regardless of what happens in the coming days.

Citizens

(Resume the chanting softly.) Svo bo da. Svo bo da. Svo bo da. *(Etc.)*

Irena

The camera pans the crowd. Moves in and across the faces. *(The candles are held close to the faces of the citizens.)*
Each one illuminated as if from within by the candle held in front of it.
I feel a stirring inside. Something struggling to get out.
Something long buried but not dead.

Citizen One

The anticipation of water behind a dam.

Citizen Two

The sudden flame coiled in a match.

Irena

I am not breathing.
(Irena speaks the words in concert with the rising chant.)
Svo bo da. Svo bo da. Svo bo da. *(All chanting stops.)*
Freedom.
The image is lost as the screen goes to black. *(The candles are blown out one by one.)*
My husband's face dissolves into the darkness.

Aslan

Svo bo da. Freedom.
When the crowd cleared, I was still alone
And Wenceslas Square can be a big empty place, if it is not your place.
There was nothing in Europe for me anymore. The defeat of communism was also my defeat.
That is when I came to Canada.
People come to Canada because they have met defeat elsewhere.
Now here is another word. Defeat. It comes from the Latin 'de' for not and 'feat' from 'faire,' to do. Not to do.

When we are defeated, it is clear we are not to do this anymore. It is time to move on.
If you wish to keep fighting, go to America. They fight there.
If you wish to move on, to not do this anymore, come to Canada.

Irena

We went upstairs but...I couldn't sleep that night.
I got up and stood at the foot of the bed.
Looking at him.
Expecting something.
I didn't know what.
Some... light.

Aslan

I turned away from all that I was, all that I knew.
It is here on these Canadian prairies, so like the plains of Kazakhstan where I grew up, that I have tried to make a home.
Only...the languages remain and in their words, my stories linger.
(He holds the book of Rilke's poems.) The poems lay on my tongue and like good wine they taste of one thing and then another. The faint memories of apple and earth flicker across my palate and run, elusive, when I try to grasp them.
I become so frustrated at times.
I carried that book of Rilke's poems with me for years, the same one your mother snatched from my pocket. I could read it and read it but I could no longer feel her hand tracing the line or hear her voice whispering the words in wonder. I could no longer bear to carry these.
I was standing very near here, I... by this river. I left it and walked away. *(He passes the book to the chorus and they slowly, reverently even, pass it down the line to Irena.)*

Perhaps it will speak more clearly to someone else.

Irena

These last ten years have been a slow reawakening. Doors opening.

Chorus

Circles closing.

Irena

It has taken me a long time to get to this place. Packing.

Chorus

We cling to our habits, what is familiar, what we know.

Irena

I have never been back to Bratislava. But Mami and Tato travel every year to a different part of the world.
Remember last year? India. Vietnam. Thailand.
They take these photographs. And Tato, everywhere he goes, he is careful to send me a postcard. In the corner of each is one colorful foreign stamp. We have never spoken of it.
I post them on my mirror.

Chorus

What was lost into the darkness, so long ago, piece by piece returns.

Irena

Oh, girl. This journey we have taken today.

Aslan

You resemble your mother.
You have her hair. Her eyes. Her...
There is nothing in you ...

of me ...
but hope.

Irena

Your father never liked poetry. For him, it was frivolous. A kind of madness.
But for me, more and more over the past few years, it has become a vessel.
A container of dreams.

Chorus

A ship to sail in.

Aslan

It is cold here.
I have been dreaming under the ice for a long time.
Looking beyond the pain into the bitter duration. Hoping for an end to winter. And here you are. My dark, winter enduring evergreen. You have cradled all that snow of grief in your hands and brought it to me like a new season. And in this penetrating light, this spring, it weeps from our fingers.

Irena

(Holding the book up.) One day about two years ago, I found this on a bench, down by the river.
It was waiting for me.*(She opens and reads.)*

Chorus

It is full of secrets.

Aslan

Tote Kinder wollten zu dir...

Irena

Dead children reach out to touch you

Aslan

O leise, leise,
tu ein liebes vor ihm, ein verläßliches Tagwerk,

Irena

Oh gently, gently, let her see you doing, with love,
some daily task

Aslan

führ ihn nah an den Garten heran

Irena

Take her to the garden

Aslan

gieb ihm der Nächte Übergewicht ...

Irena

Give her what outweighs the heaviest night

Aslan

Verhalt ihn...

Irena

Hold her. *(She closes the book.)*

Aslan

Hold him.

Irena

Your father is a good man.
But he's not the right one anymore.
I'm sorry.
I don't expect you to like it.
But I hope you will come to understand.

Aslan

Will you walk with me?
No?
Well... tomorrow. Tomorrow we will walk.
And you will tell me your story. *(There is no embrace.)*
Dovidenia.
(Exits. He leaves his son behind.)

Irena

The song.
I taught it to you when you were little. Do you remember?
Sing it with me.
(Perhaps another voice joins them. Perhaps many.)
Šípky naše sledujem
K dveram neznamym
S mojim klučom magickym
Otvorit˘ sa ich odvajim.

Šípky, šípky
Who are we?

(Black out.)

The End

Printed in the United States
32942LVS00002B/1-153

9 781896 315164